Unfinished
and other poems

Anni Macht Gibson

Published by WovenWord Press
811 Mapleton Ave.
Boulder, CO 80304
www.wovenword.com

Cover art © 2007 by Oceana Gottlieb
Cover design © 2007 by Shea Kornblum
Book design © 2007 by Vicki McVey

ISBN: 097666786X
978-0-9766678-6-5
LCCN: 2007923793

This book is dedicated to my family: husband, Jeremy; son, Drew; and, daughter Sarah-Margaret. I am grateful for your encouragement, the reading of umpteen drafts of poems and to Drew, especially, for his unfailing cheerleading, and his understanding as a fellow writer.

ACKNOWLEDGMENTS

I would like to acknowledge the following, without whom this book would not have been possible: my husband Jeremy and son Drew for their unflagging support; Sarah-Margaret for her generous help with book design; my editor, Sarah Hayward McCalla for her patient work with me and my "babies;" Kathy Wade, teacher and mentor; Sheila Dierks, my publisher; Vicki McVey, my book designer; Mary Pierce Brosmer, Bronwyn Park, Terry Pharo, and Jody Schiele for inspiration; Sally Ray, Marian Baynham, Brenda Ghantous, and Susan Bentzinger for their support; all those in my Women Writing for (a) Change writing circles for listening to my words and helping to make my writing better; and, Erin, my loyal corgi, for keeping my feet warm while I write.

I would also like to acknowledge both of my parents, Bud and Carol Macht, for being muses, in absentia. I wish they were here to read this.

CONTENTS

III. The Way We Were   77

I.

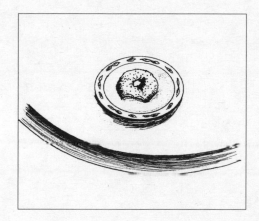

UNFINISHED

UNFINISHED

Melancholy descends like a mother-in-law
arriving unannounced,
peeking through all your cupboards,
in all your most private corners,
until you throw your hands up in disgust,
leave your bagel on the plate
unfinished,
crawl beneath the covers to hide
from the obvious transparency
of all your flaws.

The painting sits,
only pinks and mauves daubed on the canvas,
as you forget
where you put the keys to your life.
One stanza of a poem moans with loneliness,
a one-sleeved sweater sits,
knitting needles akimbo.
The linen closet's contents strewn
in the hallway attest to the fog,
descended
as you were matching striped pillowcases to sheets,
watermelon washcloths to their cousins the bath towels.

All the while, she lurks, reading your mail,
commandeering your haunts,
until there is just a tiny slice of you left,
peeping through the keyhole
watching instead of living.

Then one day, fed up, you decide to throw her out,
summon the courage to tell her it is time.
You make the plane reservations yourself,

and when she is finally gone,
you batten down the hatches,
watching the midnight lift,
sunshine melt through the house,
buttery and rich,
alighting on that morning's bagel.

Unfinished
on its blue willow plate.

You sit alone and begin to eat again.

DON'T QUIT YOUR DAY JOB

Don't quit your day job
the little voice on her left shoulder says.

Stay a waitress, pink uniform and apron
fitting a trim figure, easy to keep
with the walking and hefting of orders
for customer's tips—her favorite, the
regular who left her a twenty and told
her to go buy a condominium.

Don't quit your day job,
the insistent voice nags, nags, nags.

Be a doctor, a lawyer, an Indian chief.
Daddy says get on the payroll at the plant,
what with the benefits and all. Or go to school
to be a nurse, slapping the cold steel scalpel
into the doctor's deft and waiting hand.

Don't quit your day job,
the little voices cries,
afraid of consequences
unthinkable, unspoken.

Don't quit your day job, abandoning
the security of teaching at a school
with thirty to a class and a policy
manual the size of a small atoll.

Don't quit your day job,
to be a poet,
doing the minuet with words,
sifting through junk for the perfect phrase
to make the reader's gut zing,
or to be an artist,
transforming everyday forms
with perspective, moving her audience to tears.

Don't quit your day job
for dreams heavy with hope,
a Vegas dose of risk and the
temptation to do what you love.

Don't quit your day job?
Hah. Watch me.

LEGACY

Respectability is overvalued.
I'd rather sing deep
with the blues tattooed on my arm
than drip with diamonds and cold, perfumed fur.

Only love is real.
Masters degrees and stripes on uniform sleeves
are mirages
whether on grey flannel or dress blues.

Santa lives despite
the spate of reindeer fables, milk and cookies
munched by Dad and me,
piecing the damn bike together at 3 am.

Cats rule and dogs drool,
but they both keep you warm
when love ends
and your mattress is a mile wide.

Rock and Roll will never die.
Even with time-worn face,
your heart will still be hip
and ready to prowl like
a twenty-two year old on the make.

Death is highly overrated.
No one is happy all the time
and if they say they are,
they're lying through their teeth.
Ragged breath trumps a slab any day of the week.

ONCE, WE ALL WERE

Immigrants.
Unless
you're
Native American
and even
they
crossed
the bridge from
Siberia to Alaska
thousands
of years
ago.

Slaves
came over
against
their wills,
squalid
hulls
and
clanging
chains,
bearing
American
children,
one
of
whom
"Had a Dream."

They've
come
in waves,
Lace Curtain Irish,
Italians,
Muslims,
Jews
seeking
transformed
lives.

Pedro
comes
for
a
better life.
Minimum
wage,
sumptuous
bounty.
He
sends
money
home
to Mama
in Oaxaca
monthly.

My people
are
Johnny-Come-Lately's
from Russia

through
Poland
and
Britain,
escaping
pogroms.

All
sewn
into the
patchwork
quilt
of
America.

SAINTS

St. Joseph is buried upside down
out back so the house will sell fast.
All of the impossibles seek out St. Jude,
the patron saint of lost causes;
backwards, head turned toward the wall,
St. Anthony does his miracle thing,
if your purse just can't be located,
just pray and whisper while you do:
  Tony, Tony turn around.
  Something's lost and can't be found.

What with all these Saints running around
answering millions of prayers,
the traffic in heaven must be hell.
At phone banks, they await their peculiar ring:
St. Peter's sounds like jingling keys,
St. George's dragon roars.
Saint Patrick has his melodic harp;
Saint Ann, a baby's cry.

And on Earth, our island home,
the multitudes beseech their favorites.

Praying for answers,
a tiny light in the darkness.

HOLOCAUSTS

"Beware, do not repeat the past,"
choirs of risen souls cry out,
accused, reviled, discarded fast.
Callous crowds repress all doubt.

Choirs of risen souls cry out,
from ashes of the Holocaust.
Callous crowds repress all doubt;
cowardly hoards ignore the cost.

From ashes of the Holocaust
lunge terrors buried long ago.
Cowardly hoards ignore the cost,
hands washed clean as driven snow.

Lunge, terrors, buried long ago,
from ghettos, camps, graves en masse,
hands washed clean as driven snow,
screams still echo choking gas.

From ghettos, camps, graves en masse,
ghosts of torture emerge as one.
Screams still echo choking gas—
newly hunted begin to run.

Ghosts of torture emerge as one:
Rwandan, Christian, Muslim, Jew,
newly hunted begin to run.
Midst tears, God sees man kill anew.

Rwandan, Christian, Muslim, Jew:
accused, reviled, discarded fast.
Ghostly choirs their pleas renew:
"Beware, do not repeat the past."

PIANO SONATA

Notes dancing,
butterflies flitting in and out,
nuances of family laughing
around the dinner table.

Notes playing,
sparkling sunshine
folding into a cocoon,
fleeing disjointed despair.

Notes teasing,
saucy, impudent,
toes tickled by
lapping Lake Michigan waves.

Notes striking
silky, strong chords,
slaking our thirst,
carefully crafted crescendos.

Notes resounding,
strong, veined hands
assured on keys creating
infinite combinations of joy.

MOSAIC AT THE MFA

Japanese group with interpreter
trains eyes on Tintoretto.
An American couple wends its way,
Chinese daughter, sitting in a stroller,
almond eyes alert,
each taking in the mosaic
of men and women intent on art.

In the second floor gallery,
an octogenarian farmer gazes down
from a blue-tinted cyanatype photograph,
permanently installed in the 1970's.

With the ancients,
Egyptian dogs guard a
phalanx of pharaohs and
headless statues of Gods
and Goddesses, Ra and Amentet.

Downstairs, John Singer Sargent's
Louise Pomeroy Inches
beckons beholders,
plunging scarlet neckline,
soft alabaster décolletage.

In the museum shop,
many tired feet parade past
glass ornaments blown in Bosnia,
book after book on El Greco and Goya,

Manet, Monet and Mary Cassat,
rich reproductions of vintage
vestments and jade jewelry.

While, schooled, we scout for souvenirs
to sustain a sacred day with the masters.

CREATIVITY

Poems come from a place
so secluded that I forget
ever writing them, surprised
when I find them on my hard drive,
little presents left by God.

Science says it's the right brain process.

I know it is different
from balancing a checkbook
or writing out my grocery list,
or even from parenting or mingling
at a holiday cocktail party, dressed
in my green and red plaid taffeta skirt.

In a near trance, ideas come with words
attached like barnacles to a ship's hull,
hidden below the surface until
the poem writes itself.

I thought maybe I was crazy,
but I've heard others talk
about stories that write themselves,
characters that take on lives of their own:
the prim old maid having a fling with her sea captain,
the computer that invades its owner's mind.

My fingers fly on the keyboard,
unattached to arms or my logical brain,
as though they were kneading and braiding challah,
or, without conscious thought, weaving tapestry.

THE OSCEOLA COUNTY FAIR

The fairgrounds sleep fifty weeks a year
until, like marionettes, they come alive for show time.
Funnel cakes, elephant ears and corn dogs
waft through summer air.
Ah, the sound of arteries clogging.

Hanging out in the barns, 4-H kids
bide their time cleaning stalls. Playing cards,
like actors waiting for their scenes,
big kids stay with their heifers and goats,
little ones with perky hens or floppy-eared rabbits
in cages lined up as far as you can see,
a thousand pink noses twitching helter-skelter.

Pretty young girls painted up in sequined western gear
ride ponies—chestnuts and palominos,
ready to strut their stuff in the ring.

Blue and green, red and white, ribbons sit atop
prize tomatoes, summer squash and cherry pies;
while, in the VFW fried chicken shack Mrs. Kester
whips up another batch of cole slaw
with her prize-winning sauce.

Tomorrow, the RV's will pack up,
hitch to Ford and Chevy pickups
for the trip back to the farm.
The carnies will steal on to the next town,
wads of cash hidden under lumpy mattresses in their trailers.
And fairgoers will go home sunburned and satiated
with another year of memories of the county fair.

WOMEN'S WORK

We are wearing pinstripes
on Wall Street,
womaning the jackhammer
to tear up Broadway
between 6th and Main,
arguing cases before
Justice Ruth Bader Ginsberg.

Not that
we should go back
to the days when men
made all the decisions,
held the purse strings,
changed the oil in the car.

But where is the honor
in making the booboos go away,
organizing playgroups,
baking Aunt Ada's carrot cake recipe
from scratch,
collecting the family
for a roast and conversation
about politics and the sermon at Sunday dinner?

Who is left to gather the women in circles
to sew Wedding Ring quilts
and solve Jennie's broken heart,
Albert's row with his boss
in soft determined voices?

Where is the raucous laughter
of women with time
to chatter of everyday events,
to lift up their burdens?

Are the men doing women's work now?
Mending, convening, assuaging, feeding.

MRS. MCGUILLICODY AND THE HUMAN CONDITION

Inspired by the song "Hallelujah" by Leonard Cohen

The baby wails in a broken
Hallelujah, writhes and dies.
Mrs. Mcguillicody mourns.

Her husband's boss enters,
pink slip in hand, the end in sight.
Mrs. McGuillicody makes do.

Agnes calls, bruised ribs, broken wrist,
eyes begging for friendship.
Mrs. McGuillicody makes tea.

A canoe tips today, but
Mrs. McGuillicody carries on
stolid, even,
a row boat in the stream.

The Holy Ghost moves with her,
in the mundane actions of her day,
sweeping the front steps of her row house.

Mrs. McGuillicody goes about her work
rolling dough, amidst the neighbors' loss,
beauty in her movements, so spare.

She could slit her wrists, but there
would be no point to racing death,
so Mrs. McGuillicody waits patiently,

sets the National Geographic on the coffee table,
calico apron tied to her waist,
awaiting her own broken hallelujahs.

Her hands, veined in blue, show
the wear and tear of life.
Daughter pregnant too soon.
Son with a gay lover.

The wafer slowly melting in her mouth,
Mrs. McGuillicody seeks comfort
in the third pew on the left.

At night it's worst, the lonely truth
of life's black and white piano keys
making music for Mrs. McGuillicody,
and she weeps.

THE CURIOUS PEANUT INCIDENT

Hurtling through space
at five hundred miles per hour,
a tired looking flight attendant
offers me two packs of peanuts—
small silver sacks to savor.

I accept, almost gratefully.

Used to be, you got hot meals
on flights longer than two hours.
Now we're lucky for these peanuts.

Flying always reminds me of peanuts,
not pretzels or chips. Or even those
rich, buttery cookies one airline hands out.

Because one year my company
snatched our frequent flyer miles—
used them to cut travel costs.
No perk for long nights
far from family.

One morning,
the personnel guy came in,
found his office filled
with little packs of peanuts
airline logos on all twenty thousand.

We got our frequent flyer miles back.

Still, I think of him and laugh
when they hand out packs of peanuts.

CRAVINGS

Debonair, he rings the doorbell twice, box
tucked under his arm, wooing with chocolate.

"Melts in your mouth, not in your hands."
Who needs to market chocolate?

Dumped, mascara rivulets streaming down her face,
she takes to her bed and the comfort of chocolate.

Tiny tike, dressed as a goblin, holds his bag out
anticipating treats, not tricks. Halloween chocolate.

Behind the counter, all dolled up, she pushes truffles
at Godiva's Fifth Avenue Store. "Un peux de chocolat?"

One for me and two for you, we mix Tollhouse dough,
snarfing morsels of semi-sweet chocolate.

Anni, what makes you ever consider the possibility
of what life would be like without chocolate?

GLOBAL WARMING

God knows, this winter is
frightening for its lack of snow,
the absence of hands rubbing together
in the universal sign of cold.
Not this year,
where December and January
have tried April on for size,
ditching our temperate climate
for something more tropical.

We claim to mark time by four seasons,
but folks moan we have only two—
six months of summer, six of winter
with fleeting spells of spring and fall,
not worth mentioning but for
the occasional bijou, a jubilee,
crisp as an autumn apple,
wood smoke tickling the nostrils
or first warmth, teasing us
as we strip down to shirtsleeves,
losing layers of lambswool for linen.

They say this is an El Nino winter,
the little weather boy huffs and puffs
warm air our way, while some hope
for blizzards to keep us home
throwing extra logs on the fire,
sap jumping like popcorn.

Ambling about in light cotton sweaters
this January, I fret about the battles
my children and my children's children
will live to fight. What catastrophes can I not
yet imagine? Twenty-first century plagues:
tidal waves drowning New York,
locusts ravaging Laramie,
pestilence in St. Paul?

Feeling small and lonely,
I religiously recycle newspaper,
carry cloth grocery bags,
bemoan the dearth of public transit.

What else can one person do, save pray?

MAMA

It is our fifth spring without you,
though counting the stroke
you've been gone twelve.
My aching gut is worse, not better,
as earth turns her cycles round the sun.
No nature girl, you would have marked time
in art show openings, not seasons,
in lectures on Raphael and Mondrian,
not the blooming of larkspurs or lantana.

The one I miss is not the PhD,
who fought for workplace rights.
It is the fierce Mama tiger,
ready to protect her cub.
I miss snuggles in bed,
our last when you were paralyzed,
yet still yearned to nuzzle my nape,
to drink in the scent of your baby girl.

You would be proud of me.
I softly chant your feminist mantra,
supporting women, mindfully mentoring
expressions of joy and sorrow on the page.

Wafting in on a dream,
you are in my writing circle,
telling your story, exorcising ghosts,
sharing the tale of your granny who rocked you
when your own mother would not.

We share this cleansing ritual.
Listening, I expiate your sorrow.
You linger over the candle.
We walk to lunch arm in arm.

ATTITUDE

Knickers in a twist, hip flexed out,
who doesn't like a girl with attitude?

Be good. *Now don't you go kissin' my man!*
Gonna get you, Girl. That's my attitude.

Baby boomer, turning sixty today,
twistin' in high heeled sneakers. What attitude!

Woke up on the wrong side, back in a knot—
in your face, pit-bull-on-a-bad-day attitude.

Pretty today in a pair of fuck-me stilletos;
lusty-sex-on-a-Sunday-afternoon attitude.

Just fixed a drippy faucet all by herself.
Who needs that old man anyway—attitude?

Who's got confidence? I've got it in spades.
Don't mess with me, Honey Child. Attitude!

IDIOMS

When I'm bored on a rainy
afternoon, I lie abed poring over
Brewer's Dictionary of Phrase and Fable (1870),
filled with the origins of idioms and words of yore.

He has a bee in his bonnet,
cranky about something or other,
not to be confused with having ants
in one's pants. How uncomfortable.
Or the bees knees, which are all the rage!

So what about the son of a gun,
a bastard child in yeoman's lingo?
He's certainly not worth his salt.

Do I yearn to be a big wig, harking
back to patricians in 18th century garb?
Or perhaps I'd rather sow my wild oats,
led on a goose chase, left panting for breath.

If I ponder idioms at work too long
I'll obviously get the sack,
and be thrown back into the stone age.
No use crying over spilled milk.

No, I'd rather paint the town red
with the village idiot, and then hightail it
back to my cozy bed, at sixes and sevens,
to wonder 'bout sayings by the score.

I thank you, Master Brewer,
for giving me the lowdown
so I can make hay
with slang from your day.

WHERE WERE YOU?

*Written during the aftermath of Hurricane
Katrina destroying New Orleans, 9/05*

Winds of shame overwhelm
the boy with his finger in the dike,
"Where are you?" he says.
A wave in wolf's clothing rolls over him.

Pompeii's molten lava carries
them away. "Where are you?"
they say, floating in sewage
with the dead, deep in churlish water.

"Where are you?" he cries.
Waiting for Godot or the cavalry, perhaps.
"Where are you?" pleads the mother of
Sodom or Gomorra, rocking her dead child

as she wastes in turgid heat and filth.
The cries of thousands drown her out.
Grandpére slumps in his wheel chair
shrouded body asking "Where are you?"

Under tarps they lie, beads of celebrations past
choking the life out of them,
"Where are you?" they gasp,
mouths stretched at the tops of attics for air.

"Where were you?" we ask,
watching, from afar,
the heavy smell of death cloaking us.
"Where were you?" we ask.

"Where the hell were you?"

KNITTING

Click, clack:
unsteady needles together
break Saturday morning silence.

Steam rises off the lake:
a cold front come through
with summer's rain, rhetorical
from the great tweeded plains.

Click, clack:
trying to keep time
with the rhythm of the tiger maple
grandfather clock, ticking
against the living room wall.

Knit one, purl one:
fingers woo nubbly yarn
over and under,
a shawl,
for a Honduran woman
I shall never meet.

She has nothing
but three clay pots,
a dirt floor, love
for her four hungry children.

Each of ten thousand stitches
anticipates its job,
offering warmth
on a chilly night
in Central America.

It is a Prayer Shawl.
and I pray,
my hands working
the wool with
wobbly fingers.

Click, Clack:
Thank God,
I pray better than I knit.

FIFTY-FIVE

Soon, you'll turn the corner,
my crow's feet announce
one ordinary day.
I'd forgotten this milestone,
but the laugh lines remind me.

I am turning fifty-five.

No doubt, in October
the postwoman will deliver
a Golden Buckeye Card,
good for old-lady discounts
at the movies.

No one cards me now,
yet it seems only yesterday
birthdays were anticipated—
charmingly wrapped gifts:
driver's license at sixteen,
first legal drink at twenty-one.

I am turning fifty-five.

Now I celebrate wisdom;
vicarious victories
radiate excitement:
son settling in at school,
daughter's plum part in a play.

Deliberate, I wave goodbye
to impulsive youth, bad
relationships, careful now
who sees inside my soul.
Beauty no longer bests me.

I am turning fifty-five.

Comfortable with crafting
my third-stage self, I
hang in for the long haul,
awaiting the Crone,
a wizened sage,
chortling in her crinkled skin.

DOGS

Dogs, uncomplicated creatures.
So eager to please.

Not running hot and cold on feline whims,
stalwart companions, through thick and thin.

Labs, soft mouths ready for duty,
the Cavalier King Charles, in Widow West's lap,
.
the setter sensing seizures before they strike,
an Alsatian negotiating the rubble of 9/11.

And my Corgi who surely cogitates
thoughts deeper than her 6 o'clock meal.

A herder, counting our family members,
pouting when one has gone astray,

whose sad look betrays her when suitcases appear,
foretelling days of waiting— listless, furtive

until the herd's reunion.

And with relief upon our return,
she counts us one by one.
Her herd united, she naps, content.

INTOXICATION

You thought, perhaps,
this was a poem about
getting drunk on life,
the ruby-throated hummingbird
hovering above your head,
the salmon sunset hanging in the
Western sky, but it really is about
inebriation.

That first time, cheeks going numb
and feeling the world lift from your
shoulders, devil-may-care élan
you think is so sophisticated
as you become rickety on Minnie Mouse legs,
no longer enunciating clearly.

Or the time, after you got fired, the world
seemed a desolate place and you soothed your
soul by jumping into a martini glass
only to regret the nauseated tummy, fogged
head the morning after, wishing there were a pill.

My son wrote a story about his first time;
the Gods frowning upon him. Unaware,
a dental appointment the next day.
Imagine being poked and prodded
with pointy instruments
in a thick, hungover mouth.

And don't forget to count backwards nine months
from the birth of your first child. Chances are
there might have been a drink or two involved
conceiving more than important thoughts
in rapt conversation, tete-â-tete.

No, getting drunk is not to be recommended
by those who are familiar with the aftermath
of slipping slowly into rubber limbs and
swirly psychedelic images that wear off, alas, too soon.

Stupid? Maybe. But it's not so bad to play at once in a while.

II.

SMALL SANCTUARIES

SMALL SANCTUARIES

This dark, sleepy morning
threatens a snowy mess
quickening the pulse of poor souls
who shovel themselves to work.
The stout red dog nestles against me,
velvet ears a living rosary,
mantra for my meditation,
breathing slowly synchronized,
we sigh in mutual grace—
a small sanctuary for the soul.

Alone in the January woods,
skis and poles chat in rhythm,
tired, they pause.
Quiet briefly reigns. Then
the Nature Channel comes in
loud and clear:
woodpecker staccato,
chanting for supper
of savories under bark;
an arabesque of ice crystals
on the loamy canvas below.
Winter sanctuary for the soul.

Hectic morning, traffic honks its
dissonance, workday music.
Phone calls wait to be returned,
impatient fingers drumming.
Meetings lure me into
hours of uneasy captivity.

Competing priorities tap me
on the shoulder, insistent
babies crying for a teat.
No sanctuary for the soul.

Back to the cottage on the lake,
weekend spa for one,
tryst with my muse,
respite from daily nibbles
that drain me until I am worn
as flannel pj's, so comfy at noon,
with raisin toast and a mug of tea,
coaxing wallflower phrases
to dance in poetic communion.
Small sanctuary, revive my soul!

RENEWAL

Small towns smell of sweet connections to home,
open invitations to stop by for coffee
and a slice of Cool Whip pie that
won the Pillsbury Bakeoff in 1978.
People smile at strangers, and it makes the news
when a horse trips in the 4th of July parade,
though no one gets hurt, not even the horse.

Our pace annoys some downstate folk,
striding with urban purpose in their quest
for beaches, fudge, cherry pie.
Confident, wary, keeping score,
like the rogue wave of Eastern girls
my freshman year at college,
sorely in need of a geography lesson.
Ohio, Iowa, Illinois, homogenized,
those 4-H states, more beasts than human beings.

Decades distant, I relish the compliment, now;
achievement looks so different here.
A poem complete,
mastering the clutch on our old John Deere,
nourishing Aunt Velma with a visit
and two bowls of thick beef stew.
Imperfection is welcome, too,
honoring my weathered face,
each line and freckle a chalice of common sense.

The crisp autumn sunrise reassures me,
that striving for neon Nirvana is truly past,
traded for a porch swing, crossword puzzles
and the Volunteer Firemen's Fish Fry every May.
Cool beach sand squiggling between my toes,
I watch an ore-laden freighter sailing by,
racing to lighten her load
before the gales of November arrive.

ORDINARY TIME

Tuesday,
maybe Wednesday,
not Saturday—sleeping in.
No Sunday homily,
nor holiday Eucharist,
Aunts declaring roast beef done.
No cherry bombs exploding mailboxes,
nor picnics in the humid heat,
ants in aprons cleaning up.

Fair to middlin', I'd say.
Clouds congealed, oatmeal drab,
wondering if the weather girl ran out
of brown sugar and cinnamon.

Lights turn on, buses run,
fetching workers for deposit
in cubicles laid end to end.

Clothes
overflowing the hamper
make a break for it,
seeking absolution,
while, back turned,
I sit in
ordinary time
spinning poetry from hay.

A POET'S DANCE

Reach, en pointe,
                    arms outstretched
for the right phrase,
plucked while dipping
into an artful plié.
Twirl the ripe words

                                        throw

them skyward,

leaping

                    and catching the bunch.

Rest, on bended knee

as they alight,
                    a poem.

SNOW HAIKUS

First snow falls heavy.
Enchanted moments delight.
What kept you so long?

Squirrels dip and dive,
winter frosted bushy tails.
Cardinal perches.

Snow flakes fall lightly,
I burrow at home, cozy.
Winter warms my soul.

Perfect flakes of snow,
snuggling with one another.
Blanket for spring bulbs.

PAYING RESPECTS

"He looked real good laid out there at the viewing."
Mama told me that's what everybody says at funerals,
donning her black chiffon head scarf as we walked in.
But I didn't much believe her until I was old enough to go.

Stoic, Mama never flinched and, in time, took me in hand.

Hanky ironed, tucked up one sleeve.
Skirt, hose, shoes: dark, dignified.
Sign the book, pay respects, find a pew.
Hold hands tight, tears for us as much as them.

After, the words spilled out in line. "So sorry for your loss.
You know, they made old Harry look real good." Then we'd
run like hell for the nearest bar, for hits of bourbon, neat.
With toasts to civility and cremation,
she made her wishes known.

Mama's urn looked real good at the altar
that fractured day we said goodbye.

THE ORACLE AT THE SPA

Each day,
she waits,
gazing out
her window
on the world,
listening
for sounds
in the stairwell,
a seventeen step
pilgrimage
to the spa.

One by one,
they come
seeking solace
in the ritual,
fingernails
tuned-up,
tingling cheeks
armed for
trials of
the day,
soft feet
anticipating
sensual contact
with smooth
cotton sheets.

Deftly,
she mends
broken nails,
slipping dignity

and wisdom
among waxings,
polish and massage,
a soothing blanket
of compassion,
chamomile tea
for the soul.

One by one
they go,
replete,
unaware
of the radiant cloth
her subtle touch
weaves
of their humanity.

Each day,
she waits
at her table
by the window
in the second-floor
walk-up.
Watching
seasons change.
Waiting
for the world
to come to her.
Waiting
to heal
and
be healed.

HIBERNATION

We burrow beneath winter's blanket,
its soft gray weight
gathering each of us in its embrace—
save the crimson cardinal,
flitting from branch to branch,
home in its solstice reverie.

PICKET FENCES

In stark isolation,
we hide behind
picket fences,
pristine cages
suburban fortresses festering sin
(imagined or real) that
                                 a circle of sisters
once would have washed clean
with wisdom seen by madonnas past,
capable of embraces
to transcend the ages.

Tresses shorn,
we spin modern lives,
towers of extravagance
muting the chorus echoing
faintly...so faintly

memories of
                                 the mothers' love,
wisdom wafting
just short of our cells.

Nuclear families
are all the rage
in this age
of relocation
                                 daughters scatter
to the wind...

choosing strangers
for neighbors
instead of kin.

And we puzzle at
our isolation,
mourning what
might have been
in place of our
picket fences.

ON NOT WRITING POETRY

Didn't write a poem today.

October 23rd,
heavy with autumn's first cold,
numbing despite British tea.
Words played movie-like
across my screen,
pictures just out of focus
in that maddening way:
the smell of marble swirling,
the feel of air, not quite ripe.

Didn't write a poem today.

Did I?

ST. ANNE'S CONVENT

Generations of prayer
echo through halls
with terrazzo floors.
Reverence swirls
as the convent swells
to life with the chi of retreats
gathered amongst themselves,
the feng shui of nuns
hanging quietly in the background.
They come for solitude,
moving from self to clusters to self,
for renewal
by generations of prayers
that echo through halls
with terrazzo floors,
tranquility untwisting gnarled souls.

WEAVINGS OF LOVE

Fir trees infatuated with wind, coquettes flirting
delicate fingers waving, falling in love.

Entwined, as one, elbow to knee. The clock strikes.
Twelve. Pumpkins, on Valentines day, my Love!

Lipstick smiles on baby's belly. Mother-daughter
giggles chime. Beginning a lifetime of love.

Shiner. Broken arm. He drank again. Shit happens.
On knees he begs forgiveness. Darkest of loves.

Drumming fingers in traffic, '56 T-bird pulls up.
Ode to bygone beauty. Remember backseat love?

Slim rides into town, Cupid in disguise, six-guns for arrows.
High noon. We draw. Game, set, match. I fall. In love.

Mother God threads her loom. Copper, gold and silver.
Fiercely weaving and disbursing. Gleaming cloths of love.

ALONE AT THE LAKE

Last night, knowing you'd leave at dawn,
an ancient loneliness kicked in,
stealing my breath, against all reason.
How easily I forgot it was *my* idea to stay,
a spa for one by the frozen lake,
appointments with words on the page,
two days solid without adolescent demands.

Patiently, you prepared me yesterday,
laughing as I lay on the forest floor,
an ungainly turtle, skis akimbo.
You did not pick me up and dust me off
like my father would have, just watched
until I figured it out – thirty-five tries later,
told me I was a natural at cross-country
and reminded me to take Advil when we got home.

No coincidence, this union of ours.
Coddled only child that I was, I yearned
for freedom to fly from the yoke of perfection,
while you raised yourself,
the adults in your life distracted or drunk,
no time for a boy with his b-b gun alone in the woods.
You grew up fast, while I was fettered,
wings clipped by conscientious concern,
a suffocating love like servitude.
With you, I escaped this crystal cage.

At dawn, your confident kiss goodbye
and encouraging words rekindled adventure.
The whistling wind and rough
rollers on the bay egged me on.

So now, house asleep, I lie abed, alone,
listening to the titters of soft snow on the roof.
Excitement edges fear, an electricity
energizes me. I pad downstairs to watch
six-sided flakes perch on pillars and popples.
The cardinal keeps me company
jumping and jiving on the patio
as brewing coffee lures me from my winter reverie.
Feeling whole, the moment matches my dream of it,
and I give thanks for the freedom I've found in you.

MURDER TWO

"Suspect accused and arraigned in stabbing death of boyfriend."
She stabbed him with a kitchen knife.

She sat at the table in an orange jumpsuit,
chains confining wrists and ankles.

Murder two, half a million bail she'll never make.
Accused. Indicted. Like their relationship.

Time was they'd have a beer together
after work. Talk some, make love.

She thought they had a home in the
doublewide, her garden patch out back.

But one beer turned into five, and love
turned demeaning, unrecognizable.

Murder two. She stabbed him with a kitchen knife
when she could take not one word more.

Blood the color of the salvia outside
the trailer. Blood, red blood everywhere.

She sits at the table in an orange jumpsuit
cascading blond hair clashing with the lines of her worn face.

She takes her self somewhere else so as not to think
of the future. Murder two. She stabbed him with a kitchen knife.

Her lawyer takes her elbow as she rises to go back
to the cell where the only privacy is in her mind.

Salvia, daisies, sweet pea, snapdragons,
who will tend her garden now as she

pays the price going from one hell
to another? The price of salvia or rubies.

Murder two. She stabbed him with a kitchen knife.

THE CARDINAL

Tap, tap, tap.
Not my laptop,
but a mama cardinal,
scarlet beaked,
taupe feathers.
Circular study window
found, she can't get in
but she tries:
Tap, tap, tap.
Are you the one
who startled us,
flying frantically
round the house
two weeks ago
when we failed to
latch the back door?
Tap, tap, tap,
persistence pesters.
Stay, Mama Cardinal—
this house is not for you.

A POET'S WINTER

What is it about
January in my jammies
that produces poem after poem?
Creativity lives, as the world
outside temporarily dies,
blanketed in snow
leaves and grass dormant,
underground.

Persephone
survives
within me,
waiting,
waiting
for
Demeter
to come
calling.

Will my voice be silenced in May?

MAKING TEA

The kettle beckons
this grey February day,
one of an unending string.

Time for tea, comfort
in a cup or, even better, mug
of scalding oolong sapchong.

Tap water traipses into the pot;
I drop the stainless ball
into the mug we bought
at London's Harrods Food Hall.

While it whistles, I jump
to pluck the pan from the flame,
pour bubbling water
into the porcelain chalice
on the altar of tea-making—
striated wooden chopping block
by my sturdy stainless stove.

Strong, steeped five minutes,
luscious steaming liquid
warms my heart to life
on this flat, frigid day.

THE ROAD TO GOLGOTHA

Written for the dedication of the Chapel of the Holy Cross
Church of the Redeemer, May 2005

Two women on the blazing road,
sweat blinding their journey.
Step falling in to weary step,
loads heavy as ore
upon cumbered backs,
sore, cracked feet,
scratched shoulders hunched,
miles pass in silence but for stark echoes of travail.
Finally, Youth speaks:
 "Carry my burden this short while,
for gladly I shall carry yours."
She withers under a sunken gaze
that is the reply.
"Grandmother, are you afraid
to taste my pain. Say you
that I should shrink from yours?"
With wizened smile the Elder sighs:
 "Child, all our crosses are the same."

THE ICE QUEEN OF NEAHTAWANTA

Blank, I sit before white paper, in love with the lake,
Winter's ice queen, outside my aerie window,
guarded by fir soldiers at attention,
vigilant in dress uniforms of frost and snow.

Black squirrels, clawed prints
engrave kaleidoscopes
in the white blanket on the ground.

How can I paint this picture for you in words?

I cannot.

I should not.

So come—

see for yourself.

AUNT MAUDE

She holds her purse like Queen Elizabeth,
but has not yet perfected the imperceptible wave.
At 92, she still drives, makes wide right turns
like the long-haulers and couldn't pass
the parallel parking test if she had to.
Aunt Maude isn't about to stop now,
though once she was caught driving the wrong way
in one of those turn lanes on the strip
on the way to Joann's Fabrics, right by McDonald's.
She takes her purse to wedding receptions
of smitten young couples she does not know.
Social graces intact, she shmoozes a bit,
then sashays over to the buffet table and fills
her satchel with watercress sandwiches
and bacon-wrapped crackers to eat later,
which she never does. They calcify,
like her arteries, thoughts no longer flowing
freely on the highways of her mind.
She is past knowing.
Resigned, her daughter comes each week
to empty the purse.

DEAD SOLDIERS

Dead soldiers for drawer liners,
Mother has no lavender sachets in
the netherworld of drunks.

She did not intend it this way,
walking down the aisle in satin and lace,
but she suffocates without space for her,
silent in her world, below those more worthy—
husbands who make money and wives who
iron their men's crisp, oxford cloth shirts.

Her children's days are colored
by how she wakes, sprite-like and fresh
or hung-over in late afternoon,
destined for wintry gazes at the dinner table
or worse, bellowing over her errant ways.

She cannot leave, as luck would have it,
for he holds the purse-strings, and
the one she really wanted did not want her,
not that it really matters anymore,
with dead soldiers for drawer liners
instead of mother's lavender sachets.

Of course, life is not all dull—
once she drove "drunk as a skunk,"
they said, onto the tarmac,
boys in the back seat,
looking for Daddy's plane.
Warning signs that had been
nattering at her for years, ignored.

So what was all the fuss about
dead soldiers for drawer liners,
instead of sweet family photos
from Christmas cards pasted into albums,
along with tight shots of Florida vacations?

The black ewe, prodigal daughter,
fighting for sweet air above,
she washes away the vomit of life,
with dead soldiers for drawer liners,
sweet-talking her through another night.

PROCRASTINATION

Make a mug of tea,
add a packet of sweetener
and whole milk to taste;

check email –
respond to friends
and axe spam
that made it through;

file finished poems
in neat pocket folders
with clear windows;

make cinnamon toast,
real butter, not too dark,
sprinkle granulated sugar on top.

Sit down and
browse the thesaurus for
the "bon mot" to start with,

"indefatigable" or "unkempt,"
"vicissitude" or "vindictive"—
Word Wealth words from seventh grade.

Call to make mammogram
appointment and finally,
one for a colonoscopy.

Sharpen number two

pencils I'll never use,
given the keyboard;
sit and daydream until
the words finally flow –
a poem about not writing.

WRITING RETREAT

Anticipation sits down to the page,
pure white, neat green lines, evenly spaced,
a nosegay of number two pencils on the table
ready to scribble phrase and line.

I woke at six to the din of heating pipes,
a poem ripening in my head,
thoughts ready to jump to paper.
Images of my mother dead and gone.

It's time to sit and write
as rain pelts its percussion
upon the roof of this cavernous
convent, circa nineteen twenty.

Words wash onto the page,
visions of transgressions,
yesterday's yearnings.
A mix of memories ripples forth.

Anticipation sits down to the page
and scribbles between the neat green lines:
thoughts, evenly spaced, in poetic phrasing
as I weep for sadness and grace.

CHRISTMAS IN JULY

Crack, boom, the rain comes.

Christmas in July for the farm's dusty skin,
drinking in nectar that's been a no-show for months.
Buckwheat seeds grope for moisture
hoping to germinate, Rip van Winkle
beneath a field on the north forty,

Just yesterday we hiked, hot and sweaty
across parched acres, past shriveled watering holes,
a threatening sky toying with us to the southeast.
Like a cat teasing a mouse between her claws,
she has played with us for weeks.

Now turkeys hide in trees,
waiting for Thor's rage to pass.
Does and fawns settle on pine needle beds
on the forest floor, as rain falls steadfastly.

Quietly they wait, while earth takes her turn
opening Christmas presents from the sky.

III.

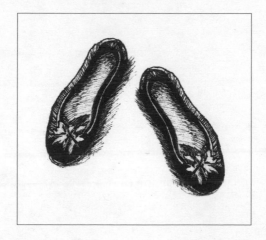

THE WAY WE WERE

THE WAY WE WERE

Both of us teens, first flight to DC,
defying Newton 'til we landed,
our destinations:
boot-camp hell and finishing school.
We came from different spheres,
but we both knew a nightmare
when we saw one, dead ahead.

"Where ya goin'?" I spit it out.
"Fort Meade, and then . . . who knows?"

I knew the code for Nam.
"Me? Mt. Vernon Summer School,"
(Pappagallo's lookin' cool).
"Gonna study how the country runs."
Learn to send boys like you to war
when I grow up to rule.

Seats 14 A and B, by chance.
John or Tom or Rick or Bill?
What <u>was</u> your name?
I swore right then, it would keep.
Now you're just a memory
in a dusty drawer of my mind.

Days flew by , touring Senate and House,
power and lights charming us all,
until, exhausted we flung off our pumps
ordered pizzas—to be delivered, no less!
This was the Big Time to Midwest girls.
You deliver to barracks, too, I bet?

It all went wrong back home, you know,
even though you weren't here
or perhaps it was *because* . . .
Burning flags and long, scraggly hair
on boys who knew better,
except Rosies didn't rivet and
Joes live in Ottawa, still.

We all wore silver bracelets then,
to keep you in our hearts,
but we really didn't have a clue.
And won't until our own are called
to defend the crisis of the day.

"Son, sit next to a pretty one,
and do not think of home
as you begin your journey."
Now a mother, I fall to my knees:
"Send him home safe,
lest a gold star come to rest
in the window of my heart."

BEST FRIENDS

The generation before me is gone,
no one left to answer questions
about crazy Aunt Evelyn,
to remind me how small I was at birth,
my head the size of a navel orange.

Who knew a best friend
would matter so much
in my sixth decade of life?
The many things only she recalls,
knitting us matching scarves
of memories from secrets
of growing up in a time
of white gloves,
crinoline petty coats,
curtsying out of respect.

Skipping in the halls,
spilling secrets along the way.
Sharing creamy whips at Coney Island.
The agony of New Math
in base two that nobody got
and Mama swore no one would ever need.
Begging to be driven to the record store
for *Rubber Soul* the day it came out.
Gym class the day JFK was shot—
teacher told us the grim news.
I laughed, thinking it a joke;
until that day, the worst we knew
was the spat between cliques
in our 7th grade class.

When Armstrong landed on the moon
at 3 am July 21st, 1969,
she was straightening her hair
as I sat on a TWA flight
from Paris to New York.
Innocents,
we lusted for Courreges go-go boots
even as evil manifested in battles
waged all round us:
struggles for equality,
our lives so black and white.

The iron curtain suffocated
the color out of entire peoples,
tanks with red-starred muzzles
pointed the way.
Napalm and agent orange
destroyed boys and jungle—
for what?
Haight Ashbury beckoned,
though we never made it there,
with flowers in our hair or otherwise.

Our lives diverged a while,
with her staying single,
teaching tots Montessori style;
me chasing glass ceilings
and ferrying the mini-van gang
to soccer games,
saccharin mall stores with
candy-flavored lip gloss,
fragrances from a cook book:

warm vanilla sugar
cranberry melon dream.

But just like Mama predicted
when we were thirteen,
we picked up twenty years later,
finishing each other's sentences
giggling over chocolate decadence,
one piece with two forks,
dessert
after a feast of sharing.
Two lives, intertwined.

LOST BOYS

First kiss, a boy named Jeff,
shy, tentative, noses in the way,
at a slumber party when the guys
stopped by in the snow, Christmas caroling.
Before you, I'd never tasted tongue.

From under the covers in
my blackened room, blue
princess phone lit up in the dark,
I invited Arlin to the prom.
You said yes, to my relief.

Two years later, Jeff shot himself.
Arlin sat on the train tracks and waited.

Please, tell me it wasn't anything I did.

BAKING PIES

My grandmother made a perfect pie crust,
flaky and sumptuous, without a recipe,
just from what was in her head,
the alchemy of ice water, flour and butter.

She was always tender with me, but she could be
sinister as a snake to my mother—
called her fat right in front of me,
when I was thirteen and Mama was forty-eight.
Nonna was eighty-one and still spare as a twig.

My mother and I baked apple pies together in the fall.
I remember the very first time—
the dough slid to the floor by accident.
I held my breath to see if Mama would get mad.
But she just picked up that wad of dough, rolled it out
and we laughed until tears streamed down our faces.

The pie came out good, too.
Not like Nonna's, but yummy anyway.
After that, whenever we made pie we slapped the dough
on the floor with a thunk—for good luck.

A little like the middle Eastern women
who weave a mistake into each rug,
because only God is perfect.

ROSA PARKS

What *was* she thinking?

Measuring hems,
taking fine stitches
with thimbled hand in 1955,
a department store
seamstress
to Montgomery's finest ladies.

What alterations
to Alabama,
the seat of segregation,
did she contemplate
that destined day?

Inquisitive, Jim Crow
peered over her shoulder.
She sat
    in middle seats
reserved for those of fated birth.

Quiet dignity
urged her to stay
when driver James Blake
ordered she stand
on worn feet,
in sensible black shoes.

"To the back of the bus."
Matter-of-fact,
he threatened
to call the police.

"You may do that,"
she rejoined, soft yet steely,
her proper grammar
and Mama's good manners
an honorable hallmark.

Ejected,
arrested,
fined ten dollars
and court costs,
courage took the reins.

Quiet icon making headlines—
erect, worthy of birthing
a movement she never intended.

"You may do that."
A dignified refusal,
the fight song of a generation
whose cup of intolerance overflowed.

LAST CONFERENCE

Once I squeezed into minute desks
chewing on my knees,
waiting for words, positive
of my children's growth,
from teachers who see
thirty kids each year.

Eagerly, I hoped for a lustrous pearl,
a tale of kindness or insightful questions,
aptitude and appetite for learning.
A mother eagle, I soared with news of grace,
readied invisible talons to pounce
should an instructor dare to raise
"opportunities for improvement."

Conferences were like buying school clothes,
proof of growth I could touch, like fine velvet;
the move from elementary to middle school,
getting beyond 6X into big girl sizes.

Years passed, the conversations evolved,
from coloring inside the lines—overrated—and ABC's
to fractions and science fair projects
until, finally, we discourse on global issues,
intricacies of anatomy and portfolio reviews:
debating slides or cd's, .j-pgs or .pdf files.

Today, I sat in chairs that fit,
for one last love-fest
for my last child, in her last year,
talking about her good eye for art—
"it can't be taught, just mined"—
how good literature shows, doesn't tell.

Yet at each weigh station along the road
I craved the same unsaid affirmation:
"You've done well, Mom,"
forgetting it wasn't about me at all.

THE JIGSAW PUZZLE

Shrill screams pierce
the fragile peace of sleep—
nagging, nagging, nagging.
Fist clenched, she slams
the fucking alarm clock
into uneasy silence.

She searches feverishly
among folds of 400 count
Egyptian cotton, gathering all
the pieces she can find,
scrubbing yesterday's
grime from each shard,
beginning her task anew.

"What is there to work with today?"
Only the familiar glances up:
titian hair, size seven feet; 10,000
freckles that want to play hide and seek
and two red cheeks, still burning with
shame from the time she peed in her
pants in Mrs. Pruden's second grade.

Working the outside pieces first, she fits
curl to curl, arms to shoulders, and legs
to feet, avoiding the jagged insides
until they shriek for attention
like brats she wants to kick
into the next county.

Resigned, she picks up memories,
conversation hearts stamped
with accusations that never disappear:
"loser" printed in the color
of her mother's voice,
dozens of scarred pieces
shouting disappointment,
tattered edges a reminder
of choices she'd rather forget.

The drill is so familiar
she could do it in her sleep,
fingertips plying curves, joints, and
recollections until she's used each and
every bit. Over and over again,
she knows how it will end before
she sees the puzzle space unfilled.

Exhausted, she crawls back into bed,
landing square upon the piece of her
that says she'll never get it right.

FINS

A late learner in the driving department,
my Manhattan-raised mother loved her boxy '54 Chevy.
But Papa made her trade it in on a "boat with fins."
She never got used to the colossal Chrysler
with push buttons for the gear shift, so moderne.
I was in the back seat when she rear-ended a Buick
right by the stately Belvedere Apartments
on the way home from Kindergarten.
The day was gloomy and the macadam wet.
Like a neophyte skater trying to stop, she slid into him.
It was all a big adventure to me: people in the street,
the police car, siren singing.
She did not find the situation amusing.
The Chrysler didn't stick around long.
Her next car was a modest station wagon. Sans fins!

MORE THAN WE BARGAINED FOR

Urban dwellers, fast food and big box stores
eluded us until Wal-Mart opened nearby.
You kids were seven and five,
the age of reason and awareness.
Excited, we loaded into the mini-van,
salivating over prices and pretty pictures
in the Sunday circular from the newspaper.

Cavernous store,
aisles towered with merchandise
eager to be plucked and placed
into the wire cart handed
us by the Wal-Mart greeter.

Notebooks anticipated classic yellow pencils,
gripped tightly by your small hands.
Elmer's glue soldiers stood in rows
with military precision, ready to paste pictures
of Asian elephants, from the National Geographic,
into fifth grade booklets on Thailand.

Toothpaste and tire gauges, bras and bathroom supplies,
decked in displays designed for us to trip over,
we wandered in awe of acres waiting to be purchased
by swarms of shoppers with carefully crafted lists.

And then, right there in the diaper aisle we saw it:

Put that back or I'll slap you, Child!
Smack, the wailing of a babe.

Guileless, you were unaware
of mothers to be afraid of.,
fathers who grimace and hit.

It happened right there in the Wal-Mart—
the loss of innocence I had to explain.

ICARUS ON A PLANE

On ascent into January heaven,
I am Icarus with engineering,
weightless droning engines.
Out the window,
floating meridian seas
above fields dressed in bridal gowns.

Undeserving, I shed pastel pink tutu:
dancing on eggshells no longer my thing.
I soar, leaving frigid life,
constricting fences like
Mother's which
encircles her heart.
I feel loss,
bitter salt and pepper in my tired hair.

Do you watch over me from above?
Or do you still turn away,
waiting for my wings to melt?

LOVE LETTERS

This came as a surprise:

My mother had a love life
before my father arrived on the scene.

It revealed itself slowly over decades:
the supplier who called on me,
delighted to find out who I was
because of Mama, the torch still lit,
burning my young cheeks
with emotion. Not shame,
embarrassment that this more-than
middle-aged man still held a flame for
my more-than-middle-aged married mother.

My parents eloped, on a whim, I suppose,
to Alexandria, Virginia, one day's drive
from Baltimore in the old Ford
Papa had bought for $200, leaky crankcase
it only started when rolling down hill.

Sentimental, Papa paid the rabbi nearly
all he had, leaving a quarter for roast chestnuts
a sumptious wedding feast. Mama went
back to the dorm while her groom, a day student,
went home to his parents' house.

Insomnia led to their demise. My Grandma,
the very soul of rectitude, wandered the halls
that night and found Mama coming out of Papa's room.
"Chilly evening, isn't it?" she quipped.
"Yes it is," my mother replied.

The marriage license was produced at breakfast.

Sixty three years later, I found the letters,
bundled in her dresser drawer,
some from the supplier,
some from my father and the ones from
a mysterious Bob—torrid, infatuated, yearning.
But by the time I found them,
she could no longer remember Bob or the supplier.
The stroke had spirited them away.

But not Papa, who stayed forever.

NIGHT FALLS

Written on the occasion of my Aunt Rita Bergson's death,
Spring 2005

The glue of life melts.
Grief rings up:
"We regret to inform you . . ."
of the last of a generation, the end of the line.

As she sails across the heavens of reunion,
a wave of sadness signs the funeral register.
Our weeping, reminiscing hearts cry out,
 "Who will speak of the days when
we were small and yours?
Who will pick us up when we fall down
and wipe away our tears?

Who, now, will testify to our goodness?"

THE 69 BUS

I.
The inclines were gone.
When I was growing up,
we rode electric buses,
rigid black umbilical cords
clutching at lifelines above,
as we bumped over
abandoned streetcar tracks
to and from town.

Ladies in hats, summer shirtwaists
and white cotton gloves;
my crinoline petticoats chafed
as I sat, skirt splayed round me
in a perfect circle,
anklets and mary-janes—
the grown up kind, straps swiveled back
to form patent leather flats.
Feeling so grown up at eight.

When the bus was crowded,
Mama made me give up my seat
for an elderly woman or one
in her eighth or ninth month;
they sank gratefully into the leatherette,
still warm from my bottom.
My skirt rustled softly
as I swayed to the motion of the bus
moving in fits and starts
towards our downtown destination.

Madison to Woodburn to Peebles Corner,
I was mesmerized by people and places
a world from my home.
At each stop, the coins made music
tumbling down the fare chute,
dark faces mingling with light
as we made our way to Fountain Square,
the center of Cincinnati. Oblivious,
I was kidnapped by thoughts of lunch
at the Windmill cafeteria,
our Saturday ritual.
Ballet class at 10, the trip
downtown for my favorite lunch.

Shrimp cocktail with tangy red sauce
that cleared my nostrils,
chocolate pudding
with whipped cream and sprinkles
and a brown and white carton
of chocolate milk which I drank
right from the container with a straw.

After lunch we'd go shopping.
McAlpin's was best for
hose, housewares, and gloves.
Pogue's for clothes and
Gidding Jenny's for Mama's occasions.
On the perfect day, Papa's charge-a-plate
would buy me a new dress—
my favorite a sleeveless,
navy-blue cotton with sailor collar
and white piping, in a big-girl size.

II.
In time, Saturday outings on the bus
became independent adventures
with friends just like me,
not hip enough to be on Pogue's Teen Board,
an honor reserved for girls who went to schools
with football teams and cheerleaders.
We wore uniforms and saddle shoes
and yearned to be cool.
A five dollar bill bought
us each a "grown up" day.
A BLT at the Women's Exchange tea room
with coins left over for a romance novel
or perhaps a new set of tortoise shell barrettes
from the notions department,
chock full of the utilitarian,
like sewing supplies and travel soap
for hand washing "delicates."

We always ended up in Cosmetics,
where wandering and perfume
samples were free.
We left reeking of cloying scents:
enough Shalimar to choke a horse.

III.
One by one, the landmarks
of my youth breathed their last.
Some, like Giddings,
where I tried on endless prom dresses,
went quietly, shutting their doors
to become fond memories. Others,

like McAlpin's fought for air
as they sank beneath the surface of suburban life.
Slowly the times changed.
Local names morphed into national chains.
Pogue's became Ayers, then May Company.
Local color lost as the comfort
of stores we'd grown up with.
Towns across America faded
into cookie-cutter sameness,
with McDonald's instead of Frisch's Big Boy,
WalMart instead of Swallens,
Oprah replacing Ruth Lyons and Paul Dixon.

One day I pulled along side
to notice none of the faces
on the 69 bus looked like mine.

Everyone I knew drove to the mall.

JANE

She was Mrs. Liebich to us girls,
the small, stern dean scouring the halls,
dark hair in a neat side-part page-boy,
lipstick vivid red, ruler in hand, ready with demerits
for the scofflaw who rolled her skirt
to a fashionable length, knees peeking
out from sky blue uniforms with box pleats.

In Modern Euro, she kept us in stitches.
Hitler's real name was Schicklegruber?
Despite the horrors, who couldn't laugh at that name?
Eleventh grade American History
weeded out the women from the girls.
No textbook, only notes.

But outside school, there was Jane,
her gutsy, deep laugh—mirth shaking walls.
She drank, too. Martinis, I discovered
the night my parents invited her for drinks.
Stunned, I saw this feared woman
had a life outside of school.
I must have thought she slept there,
in her cubby hole of an office,
grooming herself in the girls' room.

Jane and I both moved on—she to another girls' school,
I to college and life; yet, the impression she made lasts
still. Now, I know we would have been friends,
in thoughtful conversation—cozy chats about lost days,
and our class coming of age in the 60's . . .

the bad girls who did not act like ladies,
though we *were* introduced at the Silver Tea. ˙
We would have talked raising babies and growing older,
Clinique vs. Lancome to get the better of wrinkles,
how botox injections seem too painful
and surgery is just too vain.

But before we could ever talk again,
Jane died of breast cancer.

We would have so liked one another today.

SACRIFICE

I ask my mother to sing . . .
though God only knows why.
Off-key and throaty from smoking,
Mama couldn't sing to save her life.
Her voice drew my shushes
during the national anthem.

In this dream, she is different:
stable, nurturing, with a Julie Andrew's voice.
I grow up secure in her abiding love.
Here, Mama can sing . . .

but I cannot write.

INTS

I'll explain
in a minute.
But first,
I have to tell
you it is my
daughter's
eighteenth
birthday.
Today.
Now she
can vote,
or join
the army,
or get a tattoo,
without my
permission
though she
hasn't yet got
round to getting
her driver's license.
And all at once
I feel old,
because it was
only yesterday
that we were
outside in
the backyard
and she was two,
on a hot Indian Summer day,
sky cerulean blue.

She was dressed
in pink corduroy
OshKosh overalls
with flowers on
her t-shirt,
chubby
little arms
grabbing
everything she saw
and she was
fascinated
with ants,
tiny creatures
scurrying earnestly
here, there, everywhere.
Only she could
not say ant—
so they became
"ints."

THE TRIP, 1957

Twice each year, I begrudgingly let
my parents venture to Manhattan,
birthplace of my mother.

They take the train from the small, frame,
Winton Place depot;
a short ten-minute drive from our house.

Filled with anticipation,
I await their return on the platform,
looking down the long metal tracks
for the locomotive, larger than life,
so powerful it can flatten a penny—
or a little girl of five.

My mother steps down—
navy blue linen suit with white lapels,
matching high-heeled spectator pumps,
little straw hat perched on her head.
White cotton gloves shield her hands
from the grime of public places.

I see her square green train bag
loaded with gifts from that exotic place,
with no grass and buildings so tall
that only Superman can top them.

My favorite is a surprise ball:
crepe paper wound around small treasures,
to be unwrapped like a mummy
revealing a silver charm, a plastic whistle,
a doll no larger than my baby finger.

Shrieking with glee, I give belated permission
for her adventure to the big city.

A DOCTOR'S HANDS

Symbol of your life,
dedicated to saving others,
the last part of you I recognize
as you lie on your deathbed—
withered, drawn, nose beak-like,
lips dry between doses of ice chips.

Gentle hands that palpated
a belly, searching for a hot
appendix, or stroked the hair
of a cancer patient nearing the end.

Neat nails, always trimmed,
mirror of your gentleman's soul—
precise yet kind. Hands that
worried over the patient,
tenderly moved the stethoscope
across a stooped, bony back:
Breathe in, cough. Again.

Refined fingers, rough only
from washing between examinations.
Germs and infirmity held at bay.
Each day you won the battle with Death.
Small triumphs kept you going
in the face of the ones you lost.
Wringing defeats you took to heart.

Pale hands still
against the white sheet
of the hospital bed.
I drink them in, knowing each
breath could be your last.

Beside your bed,
I write this poem in
remembrance of you.

An elegy to your hands.

AUTUMN LEAVES

First leaves
drift to the patio floor,
reminders of years fallen
by the wayside, with smooth freckled
skin, and gray eyes without laugh lines. My
children grow and leave for experience
that is already mine, taking their turns,
as I walk through neat rooms of yesterday's
conversations, organizing pictures of the past.
Surely they feel the eternity of youth
as I did, then. Unimaginable, the paunch of
middle age, words that trip and trick
like déjà vu in fog. With Goddess irony, lost
on my daughter, my womb succumbs
to age just as hers comes alive,
making both of us hot
in very different ways.
It would be funny but
for the melancholy
of it all.

THE TICKET

You see it's like this,
we should not have
parked there, in the spot
with the royal blue sign,
wheelchair beckoning
my weary father,
eighty three. We were only
going to lunch, when he barked
he'd forgotten his gimpy sign
that hangs from the rear view mirror
like those domino dice
on hotrods with younger drivers
or the rosary, protecting Theresa
as she tools round town.

Patience scarcer than hen's teeth,
fireworks rang out when we found
the ticket on the windshield.
Two hundred and fifty dollars.
A king's ransom.
One to fight.
In traffic court.
Room three fourteen
of the county courthouse.
Seven p.m. Monday next.

A calico cloth of humanity,
no distinction between
rich or poor, educated, not;
right or wrong side of the tracks.
All equal before the law.

The magistrate's weary gaze testified
she'd seen and heard it all and more:
the scofflaw, nabbed, spewing excuses.
The frightened seventeen year old,
lead foot stamped on 4 tickets, one too
many to keep his license, mom by his side.

Papa stepped up to the rickety podium,
tweed jacket, felted English vest,
bow tie and carefully trimmed mustache,
still dapper and dignified, his few white
hairs neatly in place, Italian leather shoes shined.

The hard eyes softened as he spoke.
Confidently, we handed her the placard.

"Sir, this expired on your birthday in August."
Defeated, I prepared to pay our due, when
Her Honor spoke: "No, don't. Renew the sign,
I'll call the officer involved. Come back on the 24th."

On the 24th, Papa had quadruple bypass surgery.
He never recovered. At seven that night
a different magistrate, not so kind,
hard-pressed to buy my story.
She let it go, but not with out a scolding.

And me wishing Papa were still here
for more lunches, to get more tickets.

THE NANNY, CINCINNATI, 1956

Dust particles dance above a well-made bed.
The weekday afternoon begins to drain.
In quiet sun, she sits writing to Trieste
in a perfect hand that in 1920
swelled the Franciscan sisters' chests.

Stoically greeting each new morn,
her place is clear, feelings neatly
stowed among her things.
Bureau, bed, a black and white set
with rabbit ears and Joe Friday's Dragnet.
Upon the desk, her diary waits
to punctuate another day.

Expectations shelved,
her Luftwaffe lover is compost now,
the War yesterday's news.
She husbands every penny,
her pension cache.
Month to month, year to year,
initiating nothing bolder
than a frivolous night on the town
with stand-in beaux who want to make time.
Time she endures aplenty,
her only solace now caressing
another mother's child.